COOL STUFF
MAKE WITH
PAPER

Stephanie Turnbull

W

FRANKLIN WATTS
LONDON • SYDNEY

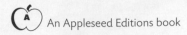 An Appleseed Editions book

First published in 2015 by Franklin Watts
338 Euston Road, London NW1 3BH

Franklin Watts Australia
Hachette Children's Books
Level 17/207 Kent St, Sydney, NSW 2000

© 2014 Appleseed Editions

Created by Appleseed Editions Ltd,
Well House, Friars Hill, Guestling,
East Sussex TN35 4ET

Designed and illustrated by Guy Callaby
Edited by Mary-Jane Wilkins

ISBN 978-1-4451-4172-5
Dewey Classification: 745.5'4

A CIP catalogue for this book is available from the British Library.

Photo acknowledgements
t = top; c = centre; b = bottom; r = right; l = left
page 1, 2 iStock/Thinkstock; 4t background Mark Hall, tr George C,
lined paper Picsfive, coloured paper Getideaka, yellow paper
bango/all Shutterstock; 5t Alexey Stiop, tl AR Images, tr Horiyan,
butterfly Quang Ho, newspaper stack Thinglass, rolled newspaper
ConstantinosZ/all Shutterstock, bananas, elephant iStock/
Thinkstock; 6l Mim Waller, r Suzan/Shutterstock, 7 Mim Waller;
8 Nata-Lia/Shutterstock; 9t Quang Ho/Shutterstock, b Mim
Waller; 10, 11 Mim Waller; 12 fofohunter/Shutterstock; 13 Mim
Waller; 14 Ivonne Wierink/Shutterstock; 15 Mim Waller;
16t djandre77, c Kichigin/both Shutterstock; 17l bonchan/
Shutterstock, r Mim Waller; 18t Anneka, b igor kisselev/both
Shutterstock; 19 Mim Waller; 20t Africa Studio, c i9370,
b WimL/all Shutterstock; 21 Mim Waller; 22 tl ruzanna/
Shutterstock, tr Hemera/Thinkstock; cl Alexander Gospodinov/
Shutterstock, bl Mim Waller, br Subbotina Anna/Shutterstock;
23 Mim Waller; 24t photomatz/Shutterstock,
b Mim Waller; 26tl and br Mim Waller, tr Zekka/Shutterstock;
27tr donatas1205, tl Kesu, c Aigars Reinholds, cartoon monster
Real Illusion, bl Bruno23, br Dorottya Mathe/all Shutterstock;
28 Maksud/Shutterstock; 30t Mim Waller, b Anneka/
Shutterstock; 31 iStock/Thinkstock
lightbulb in Cool Ideas boxes Designs Stock/Shutterstock
Cover: Mim Waller (foreground image), Dinga/Shutterstock,
Vorobyeva/Shutterstock (background images)

Printed in China

Franklin Watts is a division of Hachette Children's Books,
an Hachette UK company.
www.hachette.co.uk

Contents

Why use paper?

You can make all kinds of fantastic stuff with paper. It's not expensive or difficult to do, and you can get really creative – whether you're making cards and gifts for friends, decorations for a party, or models and **collages** to brighten up your bedroom.

Fancy folding

Many paper projects use origami, the Japanese art of paper folding. Although experts create intricate sculptures with several sheets of paper, there are plenty of simple designs to try.

You can measure and cut your own squares of coloured paper or buy special origami sheets.

Origami basics

The key to origami is to follow the instructions carefully. Make sure each fold is correct before creasing it in place – then press down firmly to make a really sharp crease. Work on a clear, flat surface with clean hands.

Cool Idea

Test out projects with scrap paper or newspaper first, so you don't waste clean sheets.

Piles of paper

Paper is such a cool craft material! It's easy to buy, but you may already have plenty at home, for example gift wrap, newspaper, magazines, wallpaper, brown parcel paper or old posters. See what else you can find!

Did You Know?

*Paper is usually made from wood **pulp**, but many other materials can be used, including grass, cotton, bananas and even elephant dung!*

Perfect planes

If you've ever folded your homework into a paper dart, you've already tried simple origami. Now you can improve your plane-making skills and impress your friends!

Ace glider

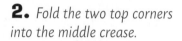

There are so many ways to fold a paper plane! Some models are copies of real planes, while others are shaped to cut through the air as effectively as possible. Here's one of the best to try.

1. Fold a piece of A4 in half longways and open it out again.

2. Fold the two top corners into the middle crease.

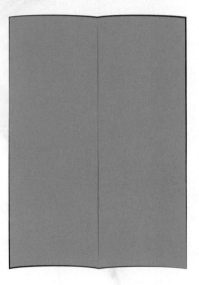

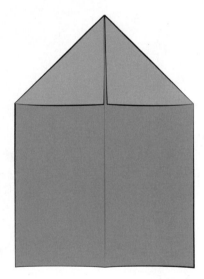

Cool Idea

Write a message inside your glider, then see if it will reach a friend on the other side of the room.

3. Turn over the paper and fold down the triangle.

4. Fold up the top point of the triangle half way. Unfold it again.

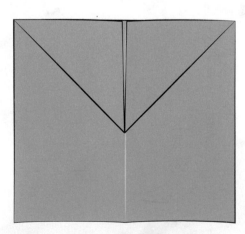

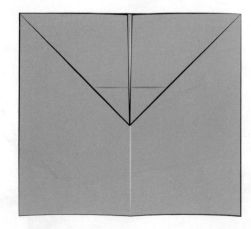

5. *Fold in the top corners so they meet in the centre, at the crease you just made.*

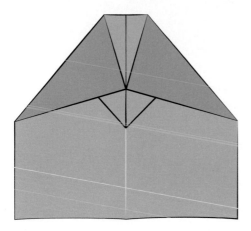

6. *Fold the top point of the triangle up again, over the corners you just folded.*

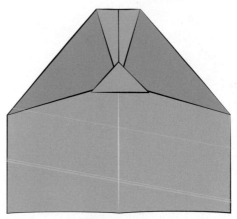

7. *Turn over the paper and fold it in half from top to bottom.*

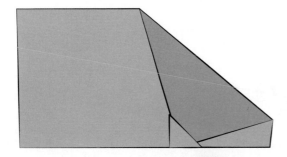

8. *Now fold down one wing so that the top, sloping edge lines up with the bottom edge.*

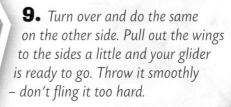

This is the edge to line up.

9. *Turn over and do the same on the other side. Pull out the wings to the sides a little and your glider is ready to go. Throw it smoothly – don't fling it too hard.*

Use felt-tip pens or colourful stickers to decorate gliders.

Did You Know?

In 2010, a plane made from paper, cardboard and paper straws was sent into space tied to a helium balloon. When the balloon popped, the plane glided back to Earth, while the camera attached to it took photos.

Origami animals

In Japan, many origami models are animals, such as cranes and butterflies, which are thought to bring good luck. They are given as gifts, hung up or used as table decorations. Why not make and display some of your own?

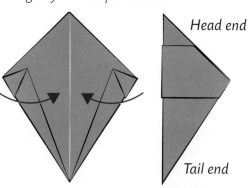

Nice mice

These mice are easy to fold and stand up well. This method uses a 15 cm x 15 cm sheet, but any size square piece of paper will work.

1. *Fold the paper in half, point to point, then unfold.*

2. *Fold in half again, using the other two points.*

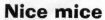

This crease is a guide line.

3. *Bring up the two bottom points to the top point. Use the crease as a guide to line up the edges.*

4. *Now fold the top points back down, so they meet the bottom point.*

5. *Turn the paper round. Take the top layer of the bottom half and fold up the tip about 2 cm.*

6. *Fold up the rest of the layer.*

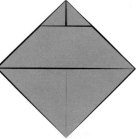

7. *Turn over the paper. Fold in each side, from the bottom point to about half way into the centre crease. Keep the bottom point sharp.*

Crease the thick paper here well.

8. *Fold the two halves together to give you a shape like this.*

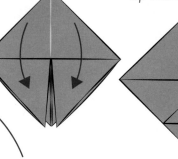

Head end

Tail end

9. *Fold the tail across the body.*

10. *Next, fold it back most of the way.*

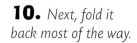

11. *Tuck the folded bit inside the main body section.*

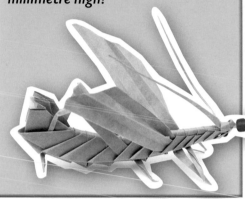

12. *Fold back the top layer of the head section.*

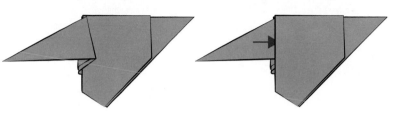

13. *Next, fold it back in half. This makes an ear. Do the same on the other side.*

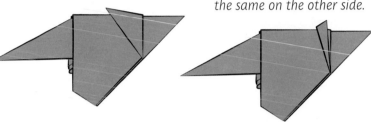

14. *Pull the sides of the body out slightly so your mouse stands up. Pull out the ears a little and curve the tail round. Add eyes, nose and whiskers with a pen.*

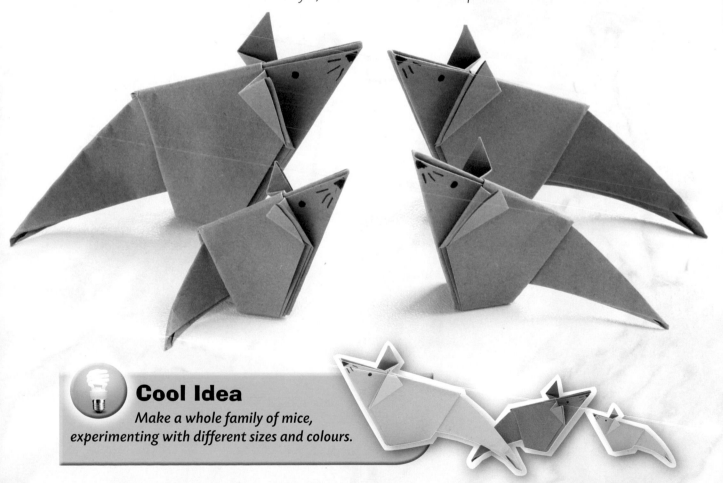

Cool Idea

Make a whole family of mice, experimenting with different sizes and colours.

Handy holders

Why not fold a pocket or box to store something special, or as a neat container for a small gift? If you use gift wrap or origami paper, start with the coloured side face down.

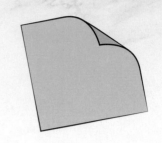

Paper pockets

A square of paper about 15 cm x 15 cm makes a perfect pocket.

1. Fold the paper in half to make a triangle.

2. Fold down the right edge to meet the bottom edge, then unfold.

3. Fold up the bottom right corner to meet the edge of the fold.

4. Now fold up the bottom left corner in the same way.

5. Fold down the top flap and your pocket is done!

You could use the back flap to close your pocket and hold it in place with a sticker.

Stylish triangles

This unusually-shaped box uses three squares of paper but is very easy to make.

1. Fold the first sheet in half to make a triangle.

2. Fold down the top left and right points to the bottom, then unfold again.

3. Fold the bottom point up, then unfold again.

4. Repeat these steps with the other two sheets.

5. Now slide the tip of the second section into the pocket created by the first.

6. Slide the third section into the second in the same way.

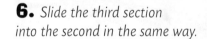

7. Keeping the lower points tucked towards the centre, slide the tip of the third section into the pocket of the first.

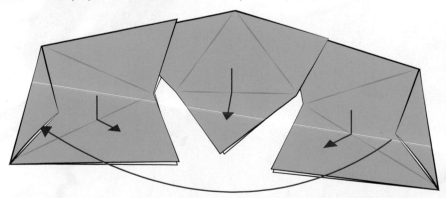

To make this box sturdier, add dabs of glue to keep the base together.

Cool Idea

Combine three differently-coloured pieces of paper to make your box, or mix patterned and plain gift wrap.

Party hats

Next time you're having a party, why not make paper hats? Provide coloured paper, felt-tips, stickers, feathers and other craft materials, then let everyone enjoy decorating their own.

Did You Know?

People wore party hats as long ago as Roman times. At a Roman winter festival called Saturnalia, everyone gave gifts, feasted and chose 'kings' to wear crowns.

Plate hats

It's simple to turn big paper plates into pointy crowns. Using a pencil and ruler, divide the flat part of the plate into eight segments, like this...

... then cut along the lines and decorate the triangles.

Clever crowns

Make a great crown with this easy method. You'll need a large sheet of paper, about 40 cm x 40 cm.

1. *Fold the sheet in half diagonally, unfold, then fold in half along the other diagonal line. Unfold again.*

2. *Fold all the corners into the centre.*

3. *Turn it over and fold the bottom section into the middle. The triangular flap should pop out from underneath.*

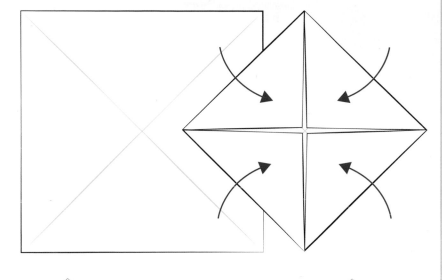

4. *Fold in the top section in the same way.*

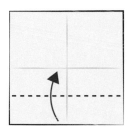

5. *Now fold the bottom triangle upwards and fold in the two bottom corners.*

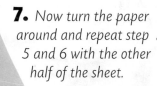

6. *Fold the triangle back down.*

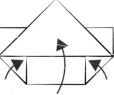

7. *Now turn the paper around and repeat step 5 and 6 with the other half of the sheet.*

8. *Open out the flaps and gently push inside to make a square hat shape.*

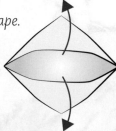

Make sure the points of your crown stand up straight. Why not add a few plastic gems?

Cool Idea
Try using thin card to make your crown – it will last much longer on your head!

Party decorations

Hats aren't the only party accessories you can make out of paper. How about creating long chains using loops of coloured paper, or folding paper diamonds over string to make bunting?

Globe garland

Use thick paper, thin card or patterned gift wrap to make this great paper garland. Choose red, gold or silver for stylish Christmas decorations, or bright orange for Halloween pumpkins.

1. *Cut out eight circles of paper, using something circular to draw around.*

Cool Idea
Get together with friends to make this garland – it will grow a lot faster that way!

2. *Fold each in half.*

3. *Glue the halves on top of each other, one by one. Keep the edges lined up.*

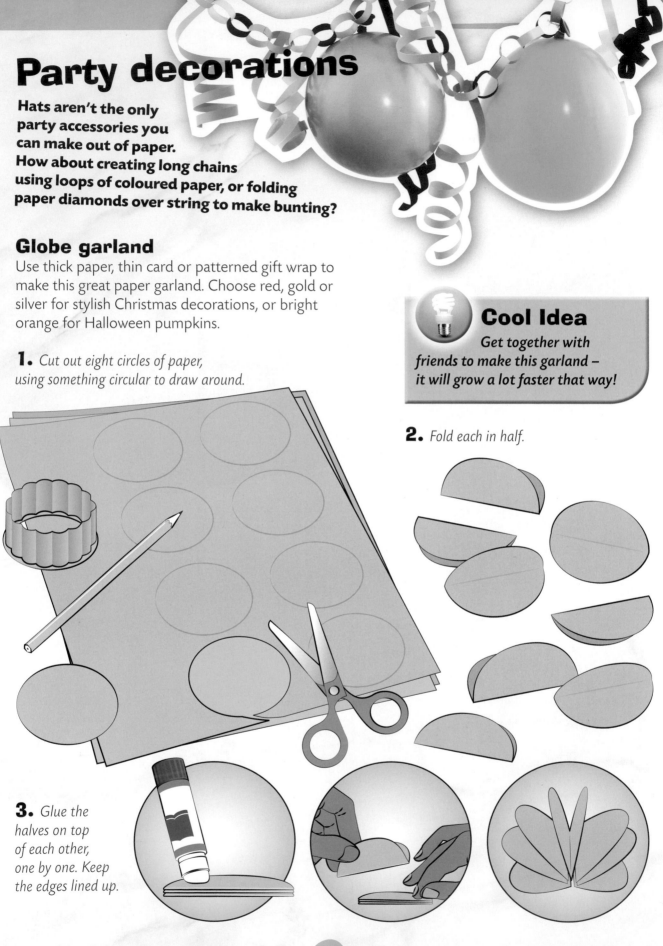

4. When they're all stuck together, run a long piece of thread, string or wool along the straight edge, then glue the top half to the bottom half to form a ball.

Leave plenty of thread loose at the end for hanging your garland.

5. Make more balls in the same way. Try alternating colours or adding stickers.

6. Loop your garland strings from curtain rails, or let them hang from the ceiling.

Did You Know?

On one day in 2005, a team of 60 people in Virginia, USA, set a world record for the longest paper chain ever made. The chain was just over 87 km long!

Stylish snowflakes

Plain white paper is perfect for striking snowflakes. Wash your hands before you start, use sharp scissors and work carefully so you keep the snowflakes clean and neat!

Basic flakes

For very simple snowflakes, take a large square of paper and fold it in half into a triangle, then in half again to make another triangle.

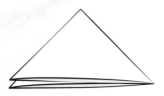 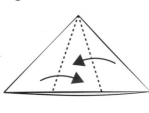 

Fold this triangle into three equal parts (thirds). Snip off the pointed ends and cut lots of little shapes into the edges of the paper. Unfold your finished flake.

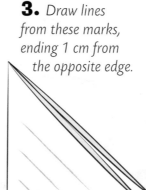

Did You Know?

*Most real snowflakes aren't exactly **symmetrical**, so don't worry if yours aren't perfect either!*

Fancy flakes

Try this clever method to make spiral snowflakes.

1. *Take a square of paper, 12 cm x 12 cm. Fold it in half to make a triangle, then in half again to make another triangle.*

2. *With the double folded edge at the bottom, make three small pencil marks 2 cm, 4 cm and 6 cm in from the left point.*

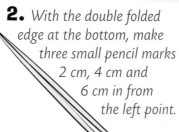

3. *Draw lines from these marks, ending 1 cm from the opposite edge.*

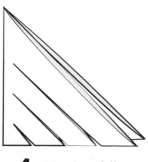

4. *Now carefully snip along each pencil line.*

5. Open out the shape, take the two smallest triangle cuts and overlap them. Fix in place with a small piece of clear tape.

6. Turn over the paper and do the same with the next two triangle cuts.

7. Do the same again, and again, to make a paper twirl like this.

8. Make five more twirls in the same way. Glue them together in the centre to make one big, beautiful snowflake.

For stylish Christmas decorations, glue on glitter and hang snowflakes in a window.

Cool Idea

Cut snowflakes with **pinking shears** to make interesting wavy edges.

Super strips

Don't waste spare bits of paper – slice them into strips and get creative! Here are three great ideas.

Paper weaving

Choose three colours and **weave** them together to make bright checks.

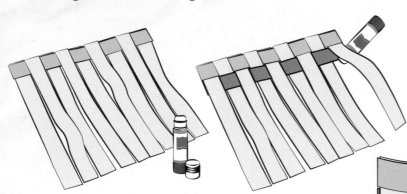

3. Add another strip, but this time go over the first vertical strip, under the second and so on. Add more alternating strips to fill the frame. Your woven square could be a flag or decoration for a card (see page 22).

1. First, glue lots of strips to one horizontal strip. Stick one underneath, the next on top and so on.

2. Thread another strip through the vertical strips, going under the first, over the next and so on. Glue it in place at each end.

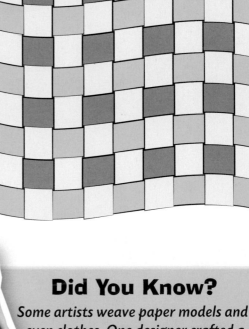

Concertina folds

To make a colourful concertina, glue two strips together at **right angles**, then neatly fold one strip over the other until you reach the end.

Glue the ends together. Add googly eyes and pipe cleaner antennae to turn it into a caterpillar, or add more strips to make a long garland.

Did You Know?

Some artists weave paper models and even clothes. One designer crafted a whole wedding dress using folded and woven toilet paper!

This dress is made entirely from paper.

Cool Idea

Use your flags to decorate party cakes or sandwiches.

Fun flags

For small, simple flags that don't need gluing in place, wrap a paper strip across a cocktail stick, like this.

Fold the end down behind...

... then fold it back across.

Turn everything over and feed the end through the loop you've made...

... then pull the strip tight and flatten the folds neatly. Trim the ends.

Cool curls

Paper creations don't have to be flat! Try curling, rolling and gluing strips of paper to make some effective 3-D designs.

Quick curling

The easiest way to curl a strip of paper is to wrap it tightly round a paintbrush handle, pencil or other cylinder, then unroll it again. This is a good way of making simple paper streamers to decorate party hats (see page 12) or gifts.

Did You Know?

The art of coiling paper strips is called quilling. Quilling experts wind tight coils of paper using special tools, then pinch them into shapes.

Loopy bird

Experiment with different colours to make this elegant paper bird.

1. Using 2 cm-wide strips of coloured paper, cut the following lengths:

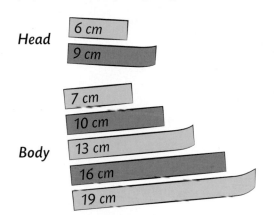

Head
- 6 cm
- 9 cm

Body
- 7 cm
- 10 cm
- 13 cm
- 16 cm
- 19 cm

Tail
- 6 cm
- 8 cm
- 10 cm
- 12 cm
- 14 cm

Beak   5 cm

Eye   3 cm

2. With a glue stick, dab glue on the end of each body strip and stick the ends together in a loop.

3. Put more glue over the join of the smallest loop and stick it inside the next size loop. Keep doing this until all the body loops are stuck together.

Make sure the joins are at the bottom.

4. Do the same with the head loops, then glue the head to the body.

5. Roll the tail strips round your finger or a thick pen to make them curl, then glue each to the bottom of the body. Start with the shortest.

6. Fold the beak strip in half. Cut it into a triangle with the narrow end at the fold.

Don't cut to a point – keep the two halves connected.

7. Fold in the ends of the triangles and glue to the head.

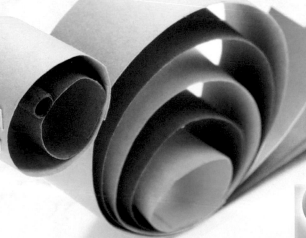

8. Finally, tightly roll the eye strip and glue to the smallest head loop.

Cool Idea
Glue coils of paper together to make a caterpillar.

Creative cards

A home-made card is far more special than a bought one — and often cheaper, too. Start with a good piece of thick card, fold it neatly, then plan your design. Here are some suggestions.

Start sticking

Glue on a square of woven paper strips (see page 18) or a pattern of neat curls (see pages 20-21). For a Christmas card, cut four circles of card as if you're making the globe garland on pages 14-15. Fold and glue them as in the original instructions...

... then stick them on your card to make baubles. Add extra shiny features such as ribbon, beads, gems or glitter.

Cool Idea

Use cut or torn paper strips to make a bright border around your design.

Pop-up rainbow

Brighten someone's day with a pop-up rainbow!
You'll need two sheets of card, each folded in half.

1. *Starting at the fold of one sheet, draw half a rainbow near the top.*

2. *Cut along the lines, then fold down the rainbow and crease well. Fold it back up.*

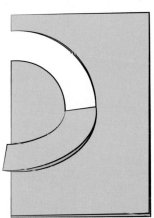

3. *Open the card and push out the rainbow flap so it folds the other way. Close the card so the rainbow lies flat inside. It should stand up when the card is opened.*

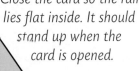

4. *Colour the rainbow and add extra decorations. Glue the paper carefully into the second card.*

Don't forget to decorate the front!

Did You Know?

Paper pop-ups were first made in the 13th century. They had flaps and turning discs that taught people about astronomy and how the human body works.

Paper piñatas

Why not make **pâpier-maché** piñatas for parties? These traditional Mexican models are hung up and hit until they break and shower you with sweets. Of course yours may look so good that you won't want to smash it!

To hang your piñata, thread wool on a *darning needle* and carefully push it down through the papier-maché at one side of the hole, then up at the other side. Do this before you tape up the hole.

Did You Know?

Traditional piñatas may also be filled with toys, dried fruit, seeds or confetti – but some 'trap' piñatas contain flour or water!

Making papier-mâché

Papier-mâché is a cheap and very useful craft material. The easiest models to make use a balloon as a basic mould. Try this funky fish piñata then experiment with your own designs. Monsters, eggs or funny heads all work well.

1. *Tear a few sheets of old newspaper into strips about 2 cm wide and 10 cm long.*

2. *Make a paste by mixing a cupful of flour and a cupful of water in a large container. The mixture should be like thick soup. Use a whisk to get rid of lumps.*

Fill the cup with modelling dough first to stop it falling over.

3. *Blow up a balloon and tape it to a plastic cup to hold it in place.*

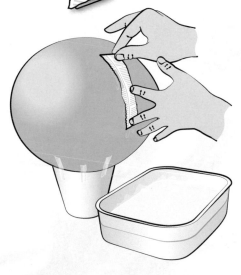

4. *Dip a strip of newspaper into the paste, run it through your fingers to squeeze off drips, then lay it flat on the balloon and smooth it down.*

Wear old clothes and cover your work surface to avoid making a mess!

5. *Add more overlapping strips to cover the balloon. Leave to dry, then add a layer of plain paper strips. (This will make your model easier to paint.) Leave to dry again.*

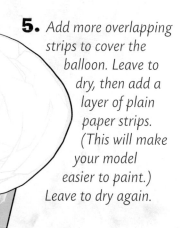

6. *Cut tail and fin shapes from cardboard and tape them on, then paint the model with bright* **poster paints** *or* **acrylics**.

7. *Snip it away from the cup and pop the balloon.*

This will be the top of your fish.

8. *Stick on googly eyes and tissue paper or* **crêpe paper** *frills. Fill with wrapped sweets then cover the hole with masking tape.*

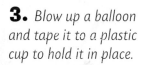
Cool Idea
Use different shaped balloons for other types of piñata. How about a wiggly balloon for a snake, or a long, fat one for a sausage dog?

Clever collage

Cut or torn pieces of paper are ideal for making colourful collages. Use them to decorate greetings cards, photo frames, party invitations and more.

Hole punch art

Use a hole punch to cut lots of tiny circles out of scrap paper, old greetings cards, magazines, wallpaper or gift wrap.
Glue the circles in patterns or use them to fill in shapes or pictures you've drawn.

*Overlap pieces of paper to create an explosion of colour, or leave gaps between each for a **mosaic** effect.*

Cherry tree collage

Hole punch circles make very effective tree blossom! Try this quick and easy design, then frame your finished picture or turn it into a card for someone.

1. *Sketch a simple tree on coloured card or paper.*

2. *Punch out lots of white or pale coloured circles. Try to get a mixture of shades.*

3. *Using a glue stick, glue the circles on to tree branches. Add as many as you like!*

Cool Idea

Use overlapping pieces of tissue paper in collages to create lots of different shades.

Magazine montage

Why not create a collage using pictures from old magazines? Make a **montage** of your favourite things, or arrange a mixture of images into a funny scene. Use the cut-outs to decorate folders or notebooks.

Check no one wants the magazines before cutting them up!

Cut out big letters to make a name plate – or a message – for your bedroom door.

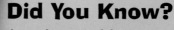

KEEP OUT OF my ROOm!

Did You Know?

The technique of decorating surfaces with cut-out pictures is called decoupage. Layers of varnish protect the paper and add extra shine.

Crazy cartoons

Why not put away the glue and scissors and get creative with just a pencil, paper and a little imagination? Here are some great ideas for fuss-free drawing.

Simple sketching

You don't have to be a great artist to create good cartoons. Keep your drawings bold and simple and add funny captions or speech bubbles to make short cartoon strips.

Doodle lots of cartoons on scrap paper, then go over the best ones in pen.

1. For a basic cartoon face, sketch two rough ovals, like this.

2. Draw eyes in the top oval and a small nose in the bottom oval. Add an ear and neck.

3. Now draw the details. Does your character have a cheeky grin or a deep frown? Are they surprised, sleepy or worried? Experiment with the position of the mouth and eyebrows to show expression.

Go over your drawing in darker pencil and rub out the sketchy lines.

Flip book fun

For more action in your cartoons, make a flip book. You need a small notebook or a pad of sticky notes and an idea for a short animated scene. How about a ball bouncing, a plane looping the loop, a chick hatching or a face changing from a frown to a smile?

1. Draw your first picture on the last page of the book, in the top corner. Keep the image simple as you'll need to draw it lots of times!

2. On the next page draw the image again, but with a slight change. It helps if you can see the first image through the paper, so you can trace over it.

Start on the back page.

3. Keep going until you fill the book or come to the end of your scene. The more pictures you draw – and the smaller the change in each – the better it will look.

4. Starting from the back of the book, flip through the pages with your thumb and watch your film!

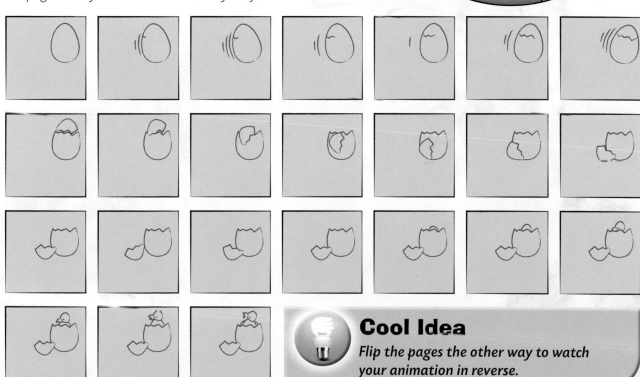

Cool Idea

Flip the pages the other way to watch your animation in reverse.

Glossary

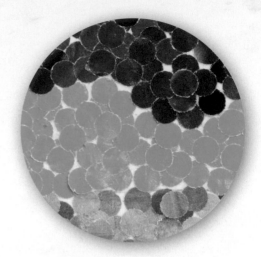

acrylic paints
Fast-drying paints that can be mixed with water or used straight from the tube. Be careful as they won't wash off clothes when dry!

collage
A collection of materials, artistically arranged and glued down.

crêpe paper
A thick, crinkled type of tissue paper.

darning needle
A long, thick needle with a large eye (hole).

montage
A display made up of lots of smaller pictures or photographs.

mosaic
A design or decoration made up of lots of small pieces of coloured glass, stone or other materials.

papier-mâché
Layers of paper mixed with paste and moulded to create models, which harden when dry. Papier-mâché means 'chewed paper' in French!

pinking shears
Scissors with blades that are serrated, like a saw, so they cut in a zigzag pattern.

poster paints
Water-based paints in lots of bright colours that are usually sold in bottles, or as powder to mix with water.

pulp
A soggy mass of wood fibres that are pressed and dried to make paper.

right angle
An angle of 90°, as in the corner of a square.

symmetrical
Made up of exactly similar parts facing each other.

weave
To lace together two sets of thread, paper or other material with one set going down and the other across.

Useful websites

www.origami-fun.com
Find all kinds of easy origami designs with clear instructions and diagrams.

www.parents.com/fun/arts-crafts/kid/easy-paper-crafts-for-your-kids
Look at a range of fantastic paper crafts including fans, mobiles, kites and papier-mâché bowls.

www.enchantedlearning.com/crafts/popupcards
Check out lots of easy ways to make great pop-up cards.

www.how-to-draw-cartoons-online.com
Learn to draw brilliant cartoon people, animals and pretty much anything else you can think of!

Index

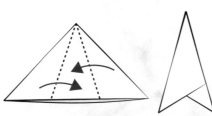